How To Succeed In A Testosterone World Without Losing Estrogen

By
Daisy Gallagher

Published By
Access International

First Edition 2012

© All rights reserved

This book is dedicated to my daughter, Lori Marie, who is my partner in business and who has taught me many lessons about what the next generation of women, when given the opportunity, will do as a positive force in the world. She inspires me every day. She is committed to our family. She has the highest professional ethics in business and is an asset to her profession and to our businesses. Most of all, she is a loving and caring daughter and a beautiful woman, inside and out.

This book is in honor of all of the women trailblazers who paved the way and those who continue to pave the way for the equality of women in and out of the workplace.

TABLE OF CONTENTS

LESSON ONE: YOU HAVE WHAT IT TAKES

LESSON TWO: DEVELOP YOUR PLAN

LESSON THREE: CONSIDER YOUR LEGAL ASPECTS

LESSON FOUR: FINANCING YOUR BUSINESS

LESSON FIVE: FIND THE RIGHT EMPLOYEES

LESSON SIX: PLAN FOR CONTINGENCY & CRISIS MANAGEMENT

LESSON SEVEN: IMPLEMENTING BEST PRACTICES

LESSON EIGHT: STAND OUT & GET THE WORD OUT

LESSON NINE: KEEPING YOUR CUSTOMERS

LESSON TEN: GIVE WHERE YOU LIVE

LESSON ELEVEN: FINDING THE LEADER IN YOU

LESSON TWELVE: GET THE HELP!

"If particular care and attention is not paid to the ladies, we are determined to forment a rebellion and will not hold ourselves bound by any laws in which we have no voice or representation."
Abigail Adams, US First Lady, 1776

PREFACE

Eleanor Roosevelt said , "You gain strength, courage and confidence by every experience in which you really stop to look fear in the face. You must do the thing you think you cannot do."

Women in business are stepping out of the box and, in spite of being in some unchartered waters, they are putting fear aside and taking that leap of faith. As the old commercial used to say, "You have come a long way, baby," but the truth of the matter is, as research proves, we are nowhere near that finish line.

Just the Facts Ma'am

To give you an example of where women are today, in 2009, The Council on Women and Girls, along with The United States Office of Management and Budget and The Bureau of Economics and Statistics Administration within the United States Department of Commerce produced the most comprehensive report on women in the history of the United States. For the first time, information from across the federal statistical agencies on five critical areas of challenges faced by women over time were linked in one research report document.

The report focused on education, families and income, employment, health, and crime and violence. The report is entitled "Women in America" Indicators of Social and Economic Wellbeing."

Here's the good news for women: the research indicates that women in America have not only caught up with men in college attendance, but younger women are now more likely to have a college or a master's degree than younger men.

Women in America are also working more and the number of women in the workforce has doubled, constituting a growing share of family income.

In 2009, the bad news is that women were still earning one third less than their male counterparts.

Because either single or divorced women with children are more likely to have responsibility for raising and supporting their children, more women in America live in poverty than ever before.

Also according to the research women are living longer than men; however, women face certain health problems, such as mobility, arthritis, asthma, depression and obesity. One out of seven women in the United States aged 18 to 64 has no usual source of health care. In addition, an increasing and alarming rate of women are victims of abuse and stalking.

> "Far away there in the sunshine are my highest aspirations. I may not reach them, but I can look up and see their beauty, believe in them, and try to follow where they lead."
> **Louisa May Alcott**

You Say *"What?"*

There were many trailblazers who came before us for women to be treated equally in and out of the workplace. The National Woman's Party thought it would be natural that the Equal Rights Amendment (ERA) would be the next step to follow the 19th Amendment providing women the right to vote. However, although it was introduced into every session of Congress from 1923 until it finally passed in 1972, it then went to the states for ratification. At the deadline, even though Congress had extended its seven year limit to 1982, only 35 states had ratified it, leaving it three short of the 38 required for it to pass.

The ERA has been reintroduced into every Congress once again and as of this writing, with the 112th Congress in session, the Equal Rights Amendment has **not** been passed, more than 90 years after Susan B. Anthony led the way for the 19th Amendment and the right for Women to Vote.

Susan B. Anthony's mark in history was shortly followed by a Quaker named Alice Paul, who started the National Woman's Party in 1917 and wrote the Equal Rights Amendment. She chained herself to the front of the White House gates and was arrested. She went on a hunger strike in jail for women to have equal rights.

In 1970, the ERA was finally passed in Congress; however, when it was sent to the states to pass, it never received enough support to be ratified within the time limit. Here we are in the 21st century still talking about rights for equality and fairness for women, as the ERA has, of this writing, still not been ratified.

In 2012, there are ONLY 72 women serving in the US House of Representatives, ONLY 17 women in the Senate and ONLY six women governors. Men hold 362 seats in the US House of Representatives and 83 seats in the Senate, and currently 44 men serve as governors. According to the US Census, as of 2011, there were an estimated 311,591,917 people in the United States, with women making up 50.8 percent of the population. There are more than 27,092,908 firms in the United States and women presently own 28.8 percent, yet only 3 percent of majority women-owned firms have revenues over one million dollars compared to 6 percent of majority men-owned businesses. As of this writing, the average revenue of majority women-owned businesses is 27 percent of the average revenue of majority men-owned businesses.

"Why" Women Are an Important Force in the US Economy

The Guardian Small Business Research Institute projects that women-owned businesses will create five to 5.5 million new jobs by 2018 – more than half the 9.7 million new small business jobs expected to be created and about one-third of the 15.3 million total new jobs anticipated by the Bureau of Labor Statistics by 2018.

Women-owned businesses already are serious players in this nation's economy. An economic impact study conducted by the Center for Women's Business Research and the National Women's Business Council documented that majority women-owned firms today are bringing in more than 23 million jobs. There is still a noticeable deficiency in employing women and providing contracts to women in science, technology, energy and math (STEM); these are the industries where the focus of a majority of the 21st century jobs will be concentrated. There is a growing momentum to encourage younger women to take up these disciplines in college.

Although the number of women-owned businesses with one million dollars or more in revenue grew 2,000 percent between 1977 and 2002 and 20 percent of all businesses over one million dollars are owned by women, it still is only at 3 percent compared to 6 percent of majority men-owned businesses.

"What" You Will Take Away

This book is written to provide you with my 30 years of lessons learned in the business world in a step-by-step method for you to evaluate, re-evaluate, plan, market and implement, whether as a new business, or an existing business stuck in the middle of the pack, or a seasoned business looking for some fresh ideas for greater success and some newfound confidence.

Starting and staying in business is challenging and intimidating, and must be maintained through strong client relationships, solid leadership, organized planning, clear objectives and lots of perseverance, faith and determination.

This is a challenge every woman business owner struggles with, regardless of the country the business is located in.

When I started my company more than twenty years ago after taking a risk and leaving corporate America, I was faced with the same challenges and filled with many questions. How do I get this started? Where can I go for help? How should I advertise? How do I get people to take me seriously? Back then, there were very few women who had taken that leap into their own businesses and the majority of the "how to succeed in business" books were written by men who had a very different style of leadership ingrained in their DNA.

I came to realize that it took a lot more time, money, effort, perseverance and patience than I originally thought. I also found that to survive and excel in what sometimes has been called "the war zone" and the hostile environment known as business can be a major hurdle for women to overcome. Business was a different and, at times, hostile environment then, and it still is to this day.

In my many years of business and being involved with different professional women's organizations, travelling to different countries and meeting other women in business, I have found that there is a commonality among women.

I have found that, as different as we all are, the majority of our gender has many of the same attributes. Ultimately, what I have found is that the innate feminine spirit is one not to be taken lightly in business. When applied properly, it becomes a strength that helps women become effective leaders. It is their compassionate nature and instinctive abilities that, when implemented into the business mindset, become secret weapons put to use by many successful women.

Women also have a warrior spirit, which is not to be confused with intention to destruct, but rather the protective nature for building bridges and creating positive change. Women have a maternal instinct that brings out the warrior to protect their child and in the case of owning their own business, often times they can transfer that maternal protectiveness to their business, employees and customers.

In the end, there is no need for women to change this structure in order to successfully lead and there is no need for women to imitate their counterparts' aggressiveness to succeed in business.

Studies have been repeatedly conducted to compare men and women as leaders. Study after study has revealed that neither is better than the other; they are just different. In some cases, women are better at reading facial cues, which is imperative in negotiations. Men hold back on their emotions; not necessarily their temper.

Women in business sometimes feel it unprofessional if they hear a story or become emotionally connected and tear up, or even cry. The fact is that female tear glands are 60 percent larger than male tear glands, so women are going to tend to cry more. Again, this may be used to a woman's advantage in the power of her leadership, as it connects people to her. Women are still negotiating as many deals as their counterparts, and in some cases, even more.

What women bring to the table is imperative and should not be taken lightly. By using their voice and empowering themselves and those around them, successful women in business have seen much positive change and there is still much left to discuss around the table. Every woman in business should insure that they and their colleagues get that seat around the table and work toward that equal playing field.

Have you wondered why it is that only a handful of women surpass their counterparts in business income? Even when making comparisons of women who, with more education, more experience and prominence in their industry than the counterpart applying for that job or contract, lose the opportunity to their counterpart, who keeps aggressively climbing his way to the top.

I asked myself these questions: Could it be the golf we don't play? Is it that the majority of us are known to retrieve from interjecting in a group setting until we are acknowledged? Is it that women on the whole are brought up in an environment to be more humble in expressing our accomplishments while our counterparts are raised not to be afraid to express and exaggerate theirs? Could it be the majority of us women are stated to take things too personally when it is only business? Is it that some of us simply burn ourselves out too early in the game because we believe success means doing it all simultaneously, by ourselves? Have we found our voice or do we readily give it up to competition?

I have been in the business world my entire adult life and I have managed to stay married to the same person for over thirty years and help raise a family. For a decade of those years, I was an employee at one of the largest international firms and got the picture of the glass ceiling.

The following two decades, I have been the CEO, chief strategy officer and founder of a corporation that started out of my home. Ultimately, this business has generated millions of dollars in revenue and contracts over the years. I have employed many people, contracted hundreds of vendors and worked with other subcontractors on hundreds of projects during the past two decades.

I have been involved in many projects and worked with a very large number of counterparts from all across the nation and abroad, from on-site to the boardroom, and I have personally witnessed scrupulous male behavior, along with supportive and indispensible male teammates. In essence, I have seen the justices and the all too frequent injustices.

Through all those years, I have served and continue to serve both the private and public sectors in the marketing communications industry and as a government contractor. These are two of the most male dominated fields of practice. I have quite a few battle scars, which I proudly wear, as they have taught me many lessons along the way. My survival – and yes, after more than two decades in my own business, it is survival of the fittest – along with my many successes and lessons learned has enabled me to survive and ultimately excel in life.

What is it that makes me and other women who have been through similar situations stick with it and keep going? Why do some of us push aside the stumbling blocks, adversities and obstacles that come our way? Perhaps it is that some of us who have hung in there see them as lessons learned rather than failures, have used those lessons to make us stronger and tend to avoid reacting the same way to those situations when they happen again.

I have found that when most people quit and walk away, it is usually the time when the answer, customer or next project will knock at the door. Many more of us have learned to use our voice for change and empowerment.

One of my favorite stories of lessons learned and those lessons put to one's advantage to complete the finish line in business, whether male or female, or in whatever project, must be given to a counterpart. In my humble opinion, there is no one else, male or female, who exemplifies the level of persistence and determination for the completion of one's vision more than Thomas Edison.

When Edison was asked how it felt to fail 10,000 before his invention of the light bulb, his curt response was, "I didn't fail 10,000 times, I found 10,000 ways how not to invent a light bulb."

Where would we all be today if Thomas Edison had not held on to his convictions and moved forward with patience and determination to finish his idea? Or if Alice Paul had not chained herself to the White House front gate or spent her entire adult life fighting over and over again for women's rights? Edison and Paul believed so deeply and were so committed to purpose that not only did they convince themselves of the ultimate success of their endeavors, they also managed to convince others to believe, invest and work for them with little or no wage in anticipation of manifesting the dream for mankind.

I am certain that somewhere along the way, someone else would have eventually invented the light bulb or written the ERA. However, it would or could have been decades later. It is this perseverance in completing a project or belief and continuing when faced with obstacles that is at the very core of every successful entrepreneur and activist.

Here is a solution for equality I dare every woman reading this book to ponder: We as women make up 50.8 percent of the population and women give birth to the <u>entire population</u> – including the other half. Women, therefore, are the first influencers with both genders. With this arsenal in hand, and when women start to

believe they hold this power of influence and use it to their advantage, women will begin to rapidly change generational perception and influence true equality in and out of the business world!

Over many years, I have spoken to women at countless conferences and seminars in the States and other parts of the world. I have spoken nationally at large conferences, internationally at the foreign ministry and had my talks broadcast over the airwaves. When I mention this simple fact and the power we hold with our circle of influence, I can hear the room buzzing with the "ah-has," and see many heads nodding in agreement or realization of this simple fact, which evades so many of us. No matter where I speak, the same thing happens.

We are the world's influencers and, as such, hold the key to the secret of writing our own future. This is probably one of the most important pieces information for women to take away from this book in the lessons learned, and one of the most difficult, as well. Women are not responsible for the restrictions that have chained us in the past; however, we can break the chains when we use our influence and our voice. No one can empower us as effectively as we can empower ourselves. Once we take onus for it, women can use and spread the power of our influence to be treated with more respect and equality in and outside of business.

We can also use our voice to not only write the policies, but also implement them and the programs into the workplace and into law. When we empower ourselves and use our voice, we create the ripple effect, which will cause the pattern of positive change for each and every one of us, not only in the United States, but around the world.

Women are learning to network better with one another and buy from other women-owned companies, or women-lead companies, yet we need to do a better job of mentoring one another; women must continue to give one another a big push up that corporate ladder in order create the bridge toward the equal playing field. Women have changed culture all across the ages. Some may think we don't have it so bad; as a matter of fact, there are more women in the workplace than ever before. We may have climbed a few steps, however; make no mistake, there are many more steps left to reach the ladder of equality.

We do not have to change ourselves to lead in business. We must change the perception of what others think and, ultimately, this begins with our own understanding of what women can and have accomplished as leaders.

At this point, I do not want anyone to think this is an anti-male book. I have been happily married for three decades to a brilliant man. It takes someone comfortable in their own skin to be married to a strong personality such as mine. I was very impressed by the manner he was brought up, to respect women as equal partners. This is a tribute to his mother, even at that time using her own voice by raising her son as a compassionate and gentle man who was not intimidated by another woman's success, nor thought twice about equality in the household.

I also owe many of my counterparts in business, politics and government much gratitude, as they nominated me for many of my awards, provided great references and have been outstanding customers of our award winning marketing communications firm.

However, I have seen the other side of the male dominated business world in many instances and experienced the bias of the unequal playing field personally, and I have many women colleagues who have also been through the same experiences.

The next lessons here are based on tools to empower women in the workplace and in business. The best way I can offer my voice is to provide the women who are reading this book with the lessons learned and the tools to strengthen your business and take you, as women, to new heights so we break that 3 percent over one million dollars in revenue for women-owned businesses, go over that less than 5 percent in contracting and, ultimately, get to the equal playing field that women have the right to hold.

LESSON ONE: YOU HAVE WHAT IT TAKES

Today, women-owned businesses generate close to three trillion dollars in sales in the United States. Women-owned businesses are growing at twice the rate of any other US business. Women now own more than 11 million firms, nearly half of the privately held businesses in the country, up from 44 percent in early 2000s. And women companies tend to be more profitable than those run by men.

Women have been stated to be less of a credit risk for bankers because research shows that women are more likely to pay on time and are more likely to stay in business.

Women Bring a New Approach to Employment

Confidence is one of the keys to success. Too often, women believe they have a stronger battle to fight because of their gender. However, they need to exude confidence and demonstrate that they are NOT the minority. Women make up 50 percent of the population and we give birth to the other 50 percent. Women have the power to change the future and are instrumental in developing that equal playing field. By being informed and using their voice to empower, women will be instrumental in ensuring their own success.

One way women are taking the world by storm is through the use of flex-time and technology, which enables more women to work from home. Flex-time and new technologies have become an overwhelming success in the bottom line for businesses throughout the country. More and more employers are realizing that some of the world's best workers have not been active due to their choice to stay home with their children. However, their choice does not mean they are not capable of being a top quality producing employee.

In a recent survey, 25,000 employees from nine large companies were asked their opinions on employee benefits. Seventy-four percent of those surveyed ranked flex-time as one of the most important. Ninety percent felt that if offered a flex-time or work-at-home option, it would positively influence their work productivity. More and more employers are realizing the importance of flex-time and home-based work options, as they recognize the strong desire for workers to balance their careers and family lives.

Employers are also realizing that they will be more likely to retain top performers by enhancing job satisfaction. So how do you approach the possibility of integrating flex-time or other home-based options into your business?

First, focus on results. Your top employees are not always the ones who put in the most hours. Be more aware of performance. Be connected to your employees. Find out what their interests are. Be in touch with their family needs, school activities and hobbies. This will allow you to understand their motivations and help you develop the most beneficial schedules and policies.

Flex-time schedules are designed to be "flexible." By definition, flex-time is "a work schedule that allows employees to work hours that are not within the standard 8am to 5pm range, while maintaining a high level of service during the organization's peak operating hours (typically 10am to 3pm)."

Offer a variety of shifts within the eight-hour day, remembering to maintain a high level of service during peak operating hours. This will allow parents to see children off to school, or pick them up, attend after school functions, tend to family needs and take part in desired activities during the week that they otherwise would not have been able to participate in.

You may also offer an adjusted lunch period. Allow your employees the option of taking up to a maximum of two hours for lunch and work later, or come in earlier if needed. This will allow people to run errands, schedule doctor's appointments or go to the gym during normal business hours.

Or allow them to choose shorter lunch periods so they may leave earlier. By offering a variety of options, you are also expanding coverage to your clients and customers, enabling them to do business with you for longer hours during the day.

Another option is offering a compressed work week. This would be characterized by an employee working a full 40-hour week in less than five days. With this option, be sure to have all days and all peak times covered.

Once you have devised a suitable schedule, keep it posted in a central location, or an online internal calendar for all employees to bookmark and view. This will make everyone aware of what departments need to be covered and who is covering them. It is up to your manager or supervisor to stay on top of making sure performance is maintained in order to ensure the opportunity provided is respected.

Overall, by offering options to employees, you will be more likely to retain and recruit top performers by increasing job satisfaction.

Overwhelmingly, companies are reporting increased productivity due to happier and satisfied employees, in turn creating happier and satisfied customers. It opens more opportunities for women (and men) to maintain their careers and balance their family lives.

"Never limit yourself because of others' limited imagination; never limit others because of your own limited imagination."

Mae Jemison, astronaut

LESSON TWO: DEVELOP YOUR PLAN

Develop Your Business/Marketing Plan
A solid plan strategy becomes a vehicle for success

A business/marketing plan precisely defines your business, identifies your goals and serves as your firm's resume. Its basic components include a balance sheet, an income statement and a cash flow analysis. It helps you allocate resources properly, handle unforeseen complications and make the right decisions. Unless you will be financing your business entirely on your own, a good business/marketing plan is crucial to obtaining any loan, because it provides specific and organized information about your company and how you will repay borrowed money. Additionally, it can tell your sales personnel, suppliers and others about your operations.

There are six key sections to your plan. The first section is the executive summary. This section will be the first part of your plan, but will be the last to be written. It is a compilation of the high points from every other section. It begins with an explanation of your company and concludes with your goals.

The second section, through careful analysis by a reputable firm, will define your company's strengths, weaknesses, opportunities and threats. It is important that everyone who is interviewed for this section is completely honest. If you start with inaccurate information, you will find yourself putting out fires you have not planned for.

The third section is your market summary. This will contain all demographic information surrounding your company. It is who is in the market for your product, what the market size is for your product and where consumers get your product or service. It will answer the questions of why the market needs your products or services and what differentiates your product or services from others. It will also outline past and current trends in your market and analyze whether or not your market is growing.

Section number four will focus on planning your strategy. First and foremost, it will declare your mission statement, outline your goals and objectives, pinpoint your target markets and plant you in a position to spread the word to those markets. In addition, it will layout the budget for your campaign.

All businesses should plan to spend at least five to 7.5 percent of gross sales on their marketing budget.

The other part to the section on planning your strategy will include customer surveys, market surveys, forecast reports and market share reports. All of these support materials will help you fully analyze your company.

The next section will focus solely on the financial aspect of your company. It should lay out your financial objectives and include expense budgets and sales forecasts. It will also offer a break-even analysis, as well as contribution margins.

Finally, being prepared means assigning responsibility and accountability. This section will detail milestones and breakdown. It will define who will monitor areas of your business. Someone should be assigned for Human Resources, Marketing/Advertising/PR, Physical Appearance, Accounting/AP/AR and any other pertinent divisions of your business.

Above all else, someone needs to be responsible for any final decisions that need to be made. You also need to have some contingency planning. Identify potential problems and have response plans in place to avoid any possible crisis. Assign specific responsibilities to division heads for these response plans.

A careful and thoroughly devised marketing plan should be the guideline for every business. A plan does not provide your company with a guarantee of success; what it does is provide your company with the roadmap it needs to begin, maintain and move the process. However, keep in mind that the best thought out plans are rendered useless if they are not implemented and allowed to sit on a shelf.

"I do not know the word 'quit.' Either I never did, or I have abolished it".
Susan Butcher, Iditarod winner, 1988

LESSON THREE: CONSIDER YOUR LEGAL ASPECTS

A Reputable Attorney Is a Wise Investment

Required licenses, zoning laws and other regulations vary from business to business and state to state. Your local Small Business Administration (SBA) office and/or Chamber of Commerce will provide you with general information. However, you will need to consult an attorney for advice specific to your enterprise and area.

You also must decide your form of organization (corporation, partnership or sole proprietorship), or tax status (e.g., should you opt for a non-profit status?).

There are several choices when forming your own business. You may run your business as a sole proprietorship, a general partnership, a limited liability company, or either a C or S corporation. Each has its own pros and cons.

The advice is that most business owners should incorporate. One of the main benefits is protecting your own personal assets.

With a sole proprietorship or general partnership, your personal assets – home, cars, financial well being – are all tied into your business and are at risk should something go wrong. By forming a corporation, you are separating the business entity from you personally and limiting that liability.

Although incorporating is more expensive than forming a sole proprietorship or general partnership, there are other advantages, too. For example, a corporation can be passed on to other people and make it easier to set up retirement plans.

Once you decide to incorporate, you need to choose between an S corporation and a C corporation. One difference between the S and C corporations is that S corporations are limited to 75 shareholders who are required to be US citizens. The S corporation also does not allow the option of offering various share levels (i.e., preferred shares). However, an S corporation provides some tax benefits.

So how do you incorporate? The process is a relatively simple one. There are many websites that offer incorporation at low prices.

The best advice is to dot all your Is and cross all of your Ts, and hire an attorney, followed by a good accountant, to make sure everything is in place. It may cost you more, but you will have peace of mind that you are starting your business right.

The attorney will prepare and file the necessary articles, as well as prepare your by-laws and minutes. He or she will make sure all proper fees are paid. An attorney can aid and direct you in obtaining your Federal Employer Identification Number and prepare a buy/sell agreement for shareholders.

After you decide to incorporate, you may need to decide on a name for the company. It should fit your business and its products or services and also indicate that it is incorporated. You will also have to name a director and/or officer(s).

"Money isn't everything...but it ranks right up there with oxygen."
Rita Davenport

LESSON FOUR: FINANCING YOUR BUSINESS

Now that you've retained a lawyer, get that accountant and get to know your banker.

Committing your own funds is often the first financing step. It is certainly the best indicator of how serious you are about your business. Risking your own money gives confidence to others to invest in your business. You may want to consider family members or a partner for additional financing. Banks are an obvious source of funds; however, the lending market is extremely difficult right now.

Other loan sources include commercial finance companies, venture capital firms, local development companies and life insurance companies. Trade credit, selling stock and equipment leasing offer alternatives to borrowing.

For example, leasing can be advantageous because it does not tie up your cash. Ask your local SBA office for information about these various sources.

Most business owners will need to consider applying for a loan. When you apply for a loan, you must provide projected financial statements and a cohesive, clear business plan that supplies the name of the firm, location, production facilities, legal structure and business goals. A clear description of your experience and management capabilities, as well as the expertise of other key personnel, will also be needed.

Initially, ask yourself these three questions:

1. How will you use the loan?
2. How much do you need to borrow?
3. How will you repay the loan?

It is a difficult balance to maintain, as you don't want to borrow less than you need. At the same time, you do not want to borrow more than you need and then find yourself stressing to make monthly payments during slow months.

The best advice I can give you is to get legal and financial advice before you sign on the dotted line. Make sure you obtain the guidance of a professional financial expert before borrowing.

This is a good time to use your attorney's counsel for review of any contractual agreements you are being asked to sign by the lender.

"Never limit yourself because of others' limited imagination; never limit others because of your own limited imagination."

Mae Jemison

LESSON FIVE: FIND THE RIGHT EMPLOYEES

Hire Right the First Time and You Will Save Down the Road

You can find hundreds or even thousands of applicants for a position through advertising headhunters, or using a workforce agency, such as Career Link. Another popular option is the use of a temporary agency. They will advertise and screen the candidates, and if the person or persons don't work out, you can have them replaced or they will send someone in their place. They will become employees of the agency rather than your company and if they work out after a certain period of time, you can usually negotiate to hire them directly. You will pay a little more, but You will save on benefits, payroll, tax, etc.

Regardless of how many people come through your door, should you choose to seek hiring employees directly. It will not matter if you do not ask the right questions during interviews, but pay careful attention to both the answer and the applicant. I found several questions that will be useful for screening applicants in a book entitled Hiring Top Performers, written by Bob Adams and Peter Veruki.

Some sample questions include:

- **Tell me about the product you are currently selling.** The candidate should be able to showcase their selling technique with this question, identifying how the product functions and what benefits it brings to its target market.
- **How much of your time is spent cold calling new accounts as opposed to servicing existing accounts?** You need to know if the candidate will get out there and bring in new clients, or is more comfortable maintaining existing accounts. Get specific information. How many cold calls each week? How many decision makers does he or she talk with? What parts of the week are set aside for cold calling?
- **How have you performed relative to your goals or quotas?** This question is all about numbers and whether the candidate is consistent in meeting his or her goals. It's also important to find out how the goals were set to see if they were

realistic for the product sold or if they were inflated or too easy to attain.

It's also important to listen to the questions the candidate asks you. When you wrap up the interview, the candidate should have some specific questions prepared about what they would like to know about your company. If the candidate tells you, "No, I think you've covered everything very well," they haven't completely prepared for the interview.

You should also watch out for the candidates asking too soon in the interview process about salary, vacation time, etc. The first round of interviews should be about discovery, the candidate learning about the job and the company, not the benefits or raises. Good questions to look for in the first round are those about the job content, and the company's culture and future.

The interview should be an exchange of information. What do you want and what does the candidate have to offer? The candidate should show an interest in the company and the kind of work you do. These kinds of questions demonstrate the investigative skills of the candidate and also that they are particular about where they work.

Questions That Should Raise a Red Flag in a First Interview:

- Questions about salary, stock options, vacation, holiday schedule, or benefits.
- Questions that have already been answered in the interview, just for the sake of asking something.

Questions That Should Raise a Green Flag in a First Interview:

- Why has the job become available?
- What is the next step?
- When will you make your selection?

Once you find the employees who best suit your company, you need to determine salary. Wage levels are calculated using position, importance and required skills as criteria. Consult your trade association and accountant to learn the most current practices, cost ratios and profit margins in your business field. You also need to consider your other financial responsibilities and what benefits you will offer your employees.

You must withhold federal and state income taxes, contribute to unemployment and workers' compensation systems, and match Social Security contributions. You may also wish to inquire about key employee life, health or disability insurance. Because laws on these matters vary from state to state, you probably should consult local information sources.

Be sure to hire the right fit for the job. Unfortunately, new startups have limited funding and mistakes are made when hiring less experienced or unqualified candidates to fill roles simply because of affordable wages. It is better to wait until you can afford to hire the best person to fit the position at the salary required than to try to fill a spot on limited funds because a project is upcoming.

Ultimately, always remember that this is your business and the employees you surround yourself with will either cause you great joy in rewards and vice versa or create havoc in the timing of your business success. The best lesson here is take your time, get professional human resource assistance if you are not

experienced as an interviewer and, most of all, do not hire with your emotions.

"A company is only as good as the people it keeps."
Mary Kay Ash

LESSON SIX: PLAN FOR CONTINGENCY & CRISIS MANAGEMENT

If you prepare for the worse scenario and hope it never happens, your business is one step ahead of disaster

Since September 11, the way we all live our lives changed forever. Businesses now need to take heightened security measures, which were inconceivable prior to that date, especially for small businesses. Extensive background checks need to be performed on potential employees, as well as customers. Your offices need to be safeguarded from any type of potential danger, as does your technology.

Crimes ranging from armed robbery to embezzlement can destroy even the best business. You should install a good physical security system. Just as important, you must establish policies and safeguards to ensure awareness and honesty among your personnel. Because computer systems can be used to defraud records as well as keep them, you should consider a computer security program. If you have a retail business, consider taking seminars on how to spot and deter shoplifting and how to handle cash and merchandise; it is time and money well spent. Careful screening when hiring can be your best ally against crime.

If you are or plan to be a government contractor, there will most likely be extra security measures that will need to be taken.

In addition, you should have a crisis management plan in place. Even the most prepared businesses often forget this essential component to the success of their firm. Many businesses don't feel the need to consider such a plan, but obstacles can happen to any business, whether big or small, metropolitan city or small town, corporate or at home. Crisis comes in a variety of forms; unless prepared, an improperly handled crisis can be one of the major downfalls of a company.

To begin, a crisis relating to your business is best defined as any event, situation or occurrence that threatens the competency, honesty, integrity and/or well being of your firm. Every business owner must be honest in knowing that crises can happen. No business is immune from such hurdles. Being aware that your business is susceptible is the first step in managing a potential crisis.

There are a few simple steps your company can take in preparing your plan.

Be prepared and anticipate a crisis. Be aware of incidents or events that may lead to one and have systems in place to prevent these possibilities, and resolutions quickly at hand if they occur. If a crime occurs, report it to the proper authorities immediately. Do not sweep it under the rug, as it most likely will come back later to haunt you and ruin your business; or worse, your reputation

Designate a crisis management team. This team should consist of key people in your company, such as your CEO and department heads. Members should also include your top PR representative (or agency) and legal counsel. All people on the team should be considered loyal associates who will lead your company through this trying time.

Choose a spokesperson(s) for your team. These are the only members who should be authorized to speak on behalf of your company. These people should be trained on what to say and how to say it effectively. Talking to the press, employees, shareholders or community during a crisis is not easy. You want to make sure the message you wish to convey is properly presented and reaches your target audience. Training will ensure that your public hears what you need them to hear.

Have notification lists readily available. Keep numbers, names and relationships with the media and press contacts current.

Keep all press materials on your firm updated. Fact sheets, bios and photos should all be up-to-date. This will help eliminate any last minute changes or mistakes in getting information to the public.

When a crisis does occur, communicate internally. Quell all rumors that generally come from within and make sure all employees are kept updated on all events. Your employees are your best source for strength and support during a crisis.

Issue a news statement. This statement should contain as much information as possible. Send the information to all media outlets and continually update them so they have the latest news directly from you and not another source. Keep the information flowing and be responsive to the media without compromising accuracy just to give them a story.

As events transpire, it is important for you to remain calm. Conduct business "as usual," maintaining a sense of normalcy while keeping your concerns and worries on the front burner. Exude confidence, but also be honest with your employees as situations occur.

If you don't already have an agency to consult, seek additional help from a reputable PR firm with the experience in handling crisis management and the development of your crisis management plan.

"Business is not financial science, it's about trading, buying and selling. It's about creating a product or service so good that people will pay for it."

Anita Roddick

LESSON SEVEN: IMPLEMENTING BEST PRACTICES

Always Do the Right Thing

It is always best to do the right thing and success usually follows; at the very least, you will sleep at night.

On average, an unhappy customer will complain to 16 people. That equals 16 potential customers your business cannot afford to lose. You also run the risk of some of those 16 people conveying the information to others. Therefore, unethical behavior in business, or not following through on a service or commitment agreed upon for a paying client or customer could mean the demise of your company.

So how can you be sure to instill or increase integrity within your business?

First, business ethics stem from your own personal philosophy. People who know you outside of your career as a person of integrity will know that your business will have the same resolve they see in your personal life.

Hire and retain personnel of integrity, professionalism, commitment to quality and fairness to others, as this is an extension of your firm and how your firm is perceived to customers. So be careful whom you hire.

As indicated in previous chapters, it is always important to develop a business plan. The more laid out your company's plan is, the stronger your image will become in the future throughout your community.

Exemplify your dependability. Make your customers aware that you are there for the long run. You want your clients to rely on you in every instance regarding your product or service.

Be totally upfront about every aspect of each product or service you offer. Hidden disclaimers and exaggerated claims should be avoided at all costs. You want your clients to trust you and by being completely honest, you will achieve your client's trust.

All ethical businesses do and should belong to various industry and business associations, including the local Chamber of Commerce, as well as professional associations within your industry, as they research their members prior to acceptance. It will benefit you as well when doing any searches for vendors, suppliers or even customers themselves to check them out with these trade associations, as well as their local Chamber.

Finally, maintain clients who possess the same level of business standards you instill in your company. The old adage is true; show me who you associate with and I will tell you who you are. A client portfolio is reflective of the type of service provider you will be working with and the same goes for the organization that is doing the hiring. Next time you have a chance, look at businesses and who they use as suppliers. I assure you that quality companies and organizations use similar types of service providers. I would also state that those who instill unethical business practices do not last too long in business, or keep customers, contracts and quality service providers.

If you are a person who follows best practices in business, your business will be on the right track for success. It's the right thing to do and the only way to stay in business in a competitive market. If you maintain an honest business and surround yourself with good suppliers and treat them fairly, they will jump through hoops for you and vice versa, and that is a path to success.

"Everything you say or do is public relations"
Anonymous

LESSON EIGHT: STAND OUT & GET THE WORD OUT

Here are the different tools for your company or yourself to be marketable

Once you have your company set up on the inside, you need to get the word out to the outside. For various reasons, it is important for every company to keep current and up-to-date information on hand. It also proves valuable to package this information into a press kit or brochure for distribution and availability to potential clients, media and investors.

There are some major components you should consider when you package your information. A reputable agency can help you determine the necessary components and how to use them effectively within the package.

The Pitch

This should be directed at your specific target audience and no more than one page in length. Ideally, it should come from your company's CEO. This letter should summarize who you are, what you do and what value you bring to the customer.

Capability Statement

It is important for your customers to know the history of your company, your capabilities and your mission. It is important to keep it as concise as possible. Attachments could be extended to include biographies of senior management within your organization relevant to the project or client's needs, and should always include a biography of the CEO and president of your corporation. In all cases, the CEO of the company must exude the brand image of the company.

Visual Imagery

Photographs or videos offer a visual reference for your clients. Photographs range from samples of a product or service you offer to photos of your team in action.

Testimonials and Awards

Be sure to include one page of quotes from clients who have benefited from your product or service and are willing to support it publicly. Potential clients are often looking for results and some form of guarantee; testimonials are proof that your product or service delivers tangible benefits.

It is also extremely important to make note of all awards and nominations your company has received. This demonstrates that you strive to excel and have been recognized for your excellence. It is also beneficial to list memberships in organizations, such as the Better Business Bureau and any Chamber of Commerce of which your firm is a member. The more organizations you are affiliated with in your field, the more credibility in your profession and colleagues you will receive. Affiliations with prestigious organizations also confirm to your customer that you are a reputable business.

Business Card

Always have a place to display your business card within your package. This offers the potential client direct contact to your firm.

Media

One of today's most viable press kit tools is a professionally designed wallet client or press kit. This should include a presentation featuring all of the aforementioned company information. This allows your customer to have an immediate interactive experience with your firm. It generates excitement toward your firm and could be the selling point if presented properly. It is much easier, when available, to develop it as downloadable from your website. It is highly recommended that you consider offering this type of presentation of your company. Consult a professional agency with the experience and technical support to develop this new media presentation.

Brochures

All of the previously mentioned items should be neatly organized in an attractive folder or brochure.

Whether you are for profit or a non-profit organization, the public will respond to materials that are grammatically correct and designed in a clear, crisp and concise manner.

You only have one chance to make a good impression. Everything you put out there to your customers is a direct reflection on the quality of service or product your company will provide. So my advice is to do it right the first time and you will benefit from your investment.

Keeping it GREEN

More and more companies are implementing sustainable standards into their marketing materials and in their companies. A recent poll showed that 80 percent of employees prefer to work for an organization that follows sustainable practices and implements these practices into their CSR.

How to Advertise Properly

Determining how to effectively advertise your business is something that requires serious thought. Because advertising is an investment, you should first decide on a budget and then develop a strategy that impacts and reaches your target audience within that budget. You want your advertising to be creative and memorable, whether it's a print ad, or a radio or television spot.

Advertising isn't just about selling your product or service; it's about selling your company. When people think of the product or service you offer, you want them to think of you, not your competitors.

There are also different reasons for advertising, so a strategy is important. You should be thematic in your approach, so your logo and company name must always be crisp and clear, and identified in the same manner. Also, in conjunction with positioning your company, there are campaigns that will necessitate advertising. Two or more mini campaigns throughout the year are usually the norm.

To begin, you need to ask yourself two questions: Where do I advertise? How frequently should I advertise?

These questions are not always easy to answer and it may take some market research and testing before you can determine which venue has the best effect on promoting your company.

Following are several advertising methods. In most cases, it is the combination of these methods with a strong message that works successfully.

Newspaper/Magazine Advertisements

Quality and placement are key to these forms of advertisements. Advertisements can be overlooked if not executed properly, or given proper placement. Research is important to ensure the newspaper or trade magazine is reaching your audience. The size is not as important as the number of runs; 4x6 is usually the rule. It is equally as important to have a smaller ad run consecutively as it is to have a full page ad run just once.

Direct Mail

This medium offers you the opportunity to reach your potential clients individually and guarantees that your company and products are seen by each person who receives your mailing. Even though it is the more costly medium, with proper research and strategy, you should reach your targeted audience. Again, direct mail is not a onetime deal. At least three times per campaign is the rule.

Broadcast

Television allows you directly access to your audience. This is a visual medium; therefore, a quality production is very important. This method of advertising does have a higher upfront production investment. This is best handled by a reputable agency, because when your company produces a catchy commercial, it could prove priceless to your business.

Radio

This medium enables you to reach a wide audience. Again, a commercial must be memorable. You need to enlist the help of an agency to research which station's audience and listening area would most likely purchase your product or service.

Repeat the Process So It Is Effective

Once you have chosen your respective medium, or a combination of mediums, your decision must be how frequently you advertise. As you or your agency strategizes your advertising campaign, you need to realize your focus. If yours is a seasonal business, it makes sense to save your complete advertising budget for one or two campaigns to kick off just prior to your season, usually about eight to six weeks prior, and run heavily through the entire season.

If yours is a year-round business, you could choose to design quarterly campaigns with a standard name recognition or institutional campaign throughout the year.

Once you've chosen your media and your frequency, how should you advertise? Most importantly, keep your advertisements simple, but effective. You want something to catch the eye or ear of your audience. That something needs to include your company name and a slogan or a jingle that is identified with your company.

Some of the most successful advertising campaigns have been focused on a slogan. These slogans automatically provide you with a product name association known as branding. These campaigns were so successful that the slogan already put the company name in the target audience's mind.

Creating a campaign around such elements as slogans and jingles, and choosing the proper frequency and venues are the keys to your success. Without proper implementation, your advertising will not be successful.

Consulting a qualified advertising agency with experience in producing successful campaigns will put you on the right track. Most agencies have teams of creative minds whose job it is to product effective advertising. They also conduct market research to determine your target audience and the best means to reach them. Their guidance could prove invaluable to your campaign and its success.

Once you have your materials designed, you need to ensure they reach the audience for whom they're intended. With markets constantly changing and shifting, it can be difficult to identify the specific target markets that are most suitable for your product or service.

Sometimes your target markets will be obvious and logical. If this is the case, start there; however, don't make the mistake of thinking your work is now complete. Potential target markets can always be more narrowly defined and tailored for your product or service. Examine your sales records and look for patterns. Can you see clusters of sales made to buyers who can logically be grouped by one or more common characteristic to form a reachable target audience?

Study your customer lists as well. Which customers are your best customers; the ones who buy the most, are easiest to reach and are best to work with? You may find that all the best customers fall into one or more clearly identifiable target market that you may or may not have been actively marketing.

When your customers place orders for your product, ask for more information, such as age, sex, telephone number, areas of interest, etc. This will make it easier to identify common characteristics among your customer base, which will be beneficial to helping pinpoint the markets you should concentrate the bulk of your promotional efforts in.

However, don't limit your product by marketing only to the same target markets again; be assertive enough to branch out to new potential markets. You can begin by looking for markets that are similar to, but slightly different than current ones. Your existing product or service and promotional efforts can probably be tailored to the new market with minimal efforts, since it will contain some shared characteristics with the old market. For example, if you are selling collection services to record clubs, why not try targeting book clubs?

Another approach to take in identifying target markets is analyzing what your competitors are doing with their advertising and promotional campaigns. Read their brochures and look at their advertisements. Their marketing efforts will reveal the markets they are selling to, markets you may want to compete for or, conversely, avoid.

Read industry trade publications for news of your competitors' sales efforts and advertising campaigns. In their desire to show off their accomplishments to the trade, your unwise competitors will frequently and unwittingly reveal their new marketing strategies to the world, and to you as well.

Get out in the consumer world and ask people for advice. Ask your salespeople which markets they feel you should emphasize in your advertising. If salespeople are successful in selling to a market you're not currently promoting in, perhaps you should consider supporting their efforts with more aggressive marketing communications to achieve even better results.

These methods will all prove very beneficial in identifying a distinct target market, thereby allowing for a more centralized and effective marketing plan. The more you know about your potential market, the better off you will be. Otherwise, you might waste a great deal of time and money implementing a disorganized marketing plan, which results from underestimating the importance of having a clearly identified target market.

Now that you have decided where your target markets lie, now you need to inform them. Timely, strategic media placement is crucial to any successful marketing plan.

You'll need to consider a number of issues to ensure successful media placement. The most important is your advertising budget. As discussed in Lesson Two, industry standards suggest that you allocate anywhere from five to 12 percent of your annual gross revenue (not profits, revenue!) to see a return on your investment.

Before designing and placing any advertisements, it is essential that you have a strong understanding of exactly what you are offering and who this product or service will be of interest to. You can obtain this information by carefully looking at the research gathered from your target market studies.

Carefully analyze your target audience and determine the best media mix to reach that audience. Ask yourself about your customers. What are their interests? What type of lifestyles do they live? What type of publications do people with those interests and lifestyles read? What television channels are they likely to watch, or what radio stations are they likely to listen to, and when? The answers to these questions will set you on the right path. You are now thinking like your customer.

Familiarize yourself with the manner in which other businesses have used the media vehicles on your list. Who else has chosen to advertise with these publications or stations? How successful have these media been for them? Try to find media outlets that include articles, programs and information materials that will compliment your product or service.

Consider the type of response you are looking to get and plan placement accordingly. Make sure there is adequate time to sell the offer, present the product and maximize the desired response. Look for venues that may offer an opportunity for some form of direct response. For example, include an address or phone number where potential consumers can obtain more information about your product, or offer a discount to anyone who mentions the advertisement.

Also be sure to consider seasonal variances that may affect the success of your advertising. The timing of your placement is crucial and the advertisement must appear when the product or service is of concern to the customer. A little common sense will help with this. If you are offering a chimney sweeping service, you don't want to be advertising at the end of winter, with spring just around the corner.

Once you have selected your desired media outlets and implemented your campaign, you must allow time, around 10 to 14 weeks, to see a return on your advertising investment. It is important to keep your name and product visible in as many areas as you can. However, it is always wise to enlist the assistance of a professional advisor to strategize your placement and media campaigns to obtain the maximum results.

Website & Social Media

In this day and age, e-commerce is an integral part of most businesses. However, there are some key areas many businesses fail to accomplish successfully when building their websites. Following are some very important areas every company should follow when considering the design of their website. Keep in mind that although the Internet is accessible to more and more customers, you must still brand your business to get customers to your door. In other words, people must know who you are before they can search your website. A website is only one small component of the promotional aspect of your marketing strategy.

First and probably most important, you should sit and plan what your needs are and what you want to accomplish. Too many people ask, "How much for a website?" That is like going into a car dealership and asking, "How much for a car?" Without knowing exactly what you need, it is hard to determine a price. However, be cautious of those ads that offer websites for $99. As with anything, you get what you pay for.

It is also important to have an expert in the field help you with the design of your website. Too many businesses try to build their own website or have "a friend" help them. This may be fine for a simple website layout, but to truly maximize the benefits of having a website, it is essential to have an expert on your side. Please keep in mind that there is a big difference between someone who "designs web sites" and a firm that offers "web design." If your website needs to be updated frequently, you are better off going with a firm that can create a back end that will allow you to easily update it yourself rather than trying to hunt down the person who designed your website every time you need to make changes.

Once you have found a firm you are comfortable with, you need to set clear goals. If you go into this venture with unrealistic goals, you will be disappointed.

Once your goals are set and you have had a chance to discuss your expectations and desires for the website, the firm's web design team will get to work putting together some design concepts for you. You should be presented with two or three initial concepts.

Next is content. You want to include what is necessary without going overboard. Too much information will only bore or confuse the visitor; keep it to what they need to know and keep it interesting. You also want to keep it appealing to the eye. Overuse of colors and fonts makes your website difficult to view.

Your content needs to be kept up-to-date. It is advisable to have someone on your staff monitor your website on a monthly basis to keep it current. News should not be more than six months old.

Websites need to entice viewers to come back and see what's new. This could be in the form of articles, newsletters, building a community with message boards/forums, or offering extras.

After you have decided the extent of your content, you want to make sure it is easily accessible on your website. Make sure links load smoothly and quickly. A visitor should be able to access every section of your site with no more than two clicks and never be forced to hit the back button.

Nothing is more detrimental to the success of your website than having a visitor log off because it takes too long for the pages to load. Also make sure that it is easy for the visitor to return to your site's homepage from other areas on the site. Larger sites go through rigid "usability" testing to ensure an enjoyable user experience.

If your website sells products online, make sure it is easy and secure for your customers to purchase directly from your site. Additionally, make sure your site is compatible with various versions of software, e.g., Netscape, Internet Explorer, etc. Test these aspects and request for a third party to review your website to tell you whether or not they found your site easy to load and navigate.

Another big mistake businesses make after designing their website is not including it in their marketing. Once you have a functioning website, it should be included in all supplementary materials. Your business stationary and every advertisement you place should include your website. Make sure your existing clients are aware that you now have a website. Give them incentives to visit the website, such as coupons, or valuable information relating to your product or service.

With over one million websites online, it is important to register yours with major search engines, like Yahoo,

Google, MSN, etc. Ideally, you want your website to appear within the first 10 to 15 results when you enter your name and location in the search line, and within the top 30 when searching for your product or service. If people can't find you, there's no point in having a website to attract new clientele.

However, search engine registration alone is not the end all. Knowing the ins and outs of each search engine is a science unto itself and is one of the reasons you should utilize the services of a professional and knowledgeable designer/firm. Most of the large search sites offer paid listings, or "sponsored listings." The benefit of these listings is that you can guarantee that every time someone does a search that contains your keywords or phrases, your listing will appear and you only pay if/when someone clicks on the link to your website.

Finally, have your website designed with a tracking tool that allows you to see which pages your visitors view most. Do not use one of those counters that you see on the homepage of many websites. This is early 90s and a professional company should not have a counter on their site. Tracking results should only be accessible by you or a designated person in your firm. Have a feedback form for areas your visitors would like improvements on, and constantly monitor and update your site.

Expand Your Brand & Marketing Budget: Sponsoring Conferences

Those who are now taking advantage of sponsorship or partnership opportunities more than ever before include government agencies, non-profits, small businesses and more large corporations.

The marketing or public relations professionals hired to develop and implement marketing communications are working with more stringent budgets and more demanding customers. The exposure from sponsorship has proven quite effective in stretching the budget.

Conference organizers usually post the sponsoring organization's logo and/or name on the conference website. The benefits of sponsorships often include a package of promotional advertisements and marketing outreach opportunities.

There are several levels of sponsorship participation. These levels should be studied carefully to insure your customer or organization is getting the most out of their investment.

Here are some questions to ask yourself when seeking to include your organization or your customer's organization as a sponsor of a conference or trade show:

1. Has the conference developed its own strong brand recognition?
2. Is the conference or trade show mission unified with your customer's mission, or, at the very least, does it provide a symbolic partnership that will place your customer in a good light?
3. Does your research indicate the conference has positive testimonials from past attendees and media coverage?
4. What is the quality of the website and the conference registration technology? How much publicity has the conference or trade show received?
5. What is the level of participation from local, state or federal government attending, and industry? Is there a global reach or audience and is it applicable to your customer? What other organizations participate?
6. What is the caliber of the previous or existing hosts, partners and sponsors?

7. What firm, if any, is handling the marketing and logistics? This is important, as the more qualified the organizing firm, the greater the chances of success for your customer's outreach.
8. What perks are being offered to your customer if they sponsor? Does your customer have an opportunity to connect with other sponsors at a private reception or other welcoming session?
9. Are the organizers open to your assistance in bringing or highlighting the connection between your customer and the organization?
10. What is the agenda? What are the qualification requirements for vetting speakers? This is extremely important, as the more stringent requirements for vetting speakers equals more solid topics and substance, which is critical to the success of conferences. Is there an opportunity for your customer, if qualified based on criteria, to speak or moderate a session if applicable to the audience?

These are just a few of the questions to ask in research and moving forward in sponsoring or exhibiting at conferences. The additional benefit for your customer or any organization is the opportunity to network and meet potential or existing customers. For marketing professionals who have large businesses as customers, they should look for conferences that have a similar level of participation along with global and top government leaders.

For small businesses, they should not only look to attend or sponsor small business conferences, they should also look for opportunities to participate in the larger conferences where connecting with government agencies and/or prime contractors are more prevalent, as well as open doors for more networking and outreaching for subcontracting opportunities with large agencies and large companies.

Keep all avenues and your budget in perspective, and maintain your customer's or organization's mission and brand integrity in mind when associating conference sponsorships for outreach.

Once you have committed to the sponsorship of a high profile conference or trade show, also do your part to spread the word to insure more attendance. Send a press release out to your local media, send an email blast to your customer's colleagues and clients and post on their social media accounts and websites so others are aware of your participation and can provide you with an opportunity to link with other likeminded brands.

LESSON NINE: KEEPING YOUR CUSTOMERS

The most important customer to attract is the one you already have

Once your business begins to grow, you need to concentrate on maintaining your relationships with your existing clients. Often times, businesses expend enormous resources on attracting new customers and lack putting sufficient effort into increasing revenue by keeping those they already have happy through customer loyalty programs and incentives.

This is a vital step in business growth and it is too often overlooked. Studies show that on average, it can cost five to six times more for a company to attract a new customer than keep an existing one. Try evaluating your customer base. You may discover that the top 20 percent of your clients give you 80 percent of your profits. It is for this reason that creating and implementing a customer loyalty plan should be a top priority for all business owners.

So how do you begin? First, you need to look for a program that is cost effective and easy to manage.

You will want to begin by examining your current marketing strategies. Aside from excelling in customer service and always being available to your clients, you want your marketing strategy to help you identify, retain and grow your top clients. You can achieve success with this strategy by communicating with your customers through targeted messages that speak directly to them and address their specific needs.

Constantly reaching out to your customers makes them feel important; reaching out to them and making them feel like you know who they are is even better. The more you know about each of your clients individually, the better your chances are of retaining them. This works well for a small retail or service enterprise; larger firms need promotional tools and incentives because of the obvious lack of interpersonal relationships at that level.

There are many ways to achieve personal relationships between your clients and your company. Many firms assign a specific representative for each client and create databases with detailed information. Sending holiday or birthday cards and newsletters are also effective ways to continue the constant contact required to maintain your clients. If your current strategy does not include steps like these to help you achieve these elements, you should restructure your plan to help you establish relationships with your clients.

No matter how you choose to structure your marketing strategy, your plan should include a reward or incentive program targeted to your existing clients or customers.

Reward or incentive programs can work in a variety of ways. You can implement any of the following ideas or programs into your plan:

1. In retail, you can offer special sales and special hours just to your best customers. This will make your clients feel like they are being rewarded for being your customers and, in turn, increase your sales by having them "shop" at special hours when the store is not crowded and they can get the salesperson's undivided attention. Or creating a VIP discount card for long-standing customers is a good incentive program. A fixed discount will automatically be deducted every time they purchase goods or services from you and you will be able to track the purchases and ROI on this incentive.

2. Offer discounts to clients as a thank you for being a good customer. Small businesses on small budgets can increase customer loyalty, but offer a

discount on a service that your customer doesn't ordinarily use. For instance, if you own a beauty salon and you have a client who always comes to you for a haircut, you may want to offer her a discount on a perm or coloring. This will ensure that she or he will continue to come to you for their haircut, but it will also introduce the client to a different service they may choose to continue.

3. Offer special gifts or free items to customers who come into your store or company on a certain day. They will be coming in for their free gift, but, in turn, may end up finding something else to purchase. Also, if you have a service business, such as a marketing or legal firm, and your client has a large retainer or contract with you, offer them something at no cost as a thank you. For example, an ad or press release for marketing firms at no cost helps introduce your customer to a potential new service. These rewards and special attention means a great deal to a loyal client. In most cases, it is the thought that means even more than the discount.

4. Offer a point reward program. This type of program has become increasingly popular in

recent years. Customers receive points for every dollar they spend on your products or services. Points are then either converted to dollars, as in Discover Card's cash back reward program, or they can be accumulated to earn free gifts or vacations. This encourages your customers to spend more money to reach the level they desire.

By implementing any of the above into your marketing plan, you are taking a big step in guaranteeing a high rate of customer retention and loyalty. Your existing customers are your most valuable assets. According to the Harvard Business Review, achieving a 5 percent increase in customer retention can increase your profits by nearly 100 percent. The above plans will help you develop ways to not only retain your customers, but to reward and thank them for choosing you as their provider.

By nature, people want to feel they are appreciated when they buy a product or service. The proverbial thank you still goes a long way. In the end, the foundation of your company's success is based on the service you provide your long-standing customers. If you keep your existing customers happy, they will increase the business they bring to your door. I guarantee you will also find they will bring other business to your door as well. A loyal customer is by far your best marketing tool.

LESSON TEN: GIVE WHERE YOU LIVE

As it is important to maintain relationships with your clients, it is equally as important to develop and maintain relationships within your community.

Today's society demands that corporations be socially responsible and active within the community. The community, not the government, grants corporations their licenses to operate. Because of this, community relations has become increasingly important, as well as mutually beneficial to both the community and the corporation.

From the company's side, a good corporate neighbor policy improves internal morale and assists with recruitment and retainment of personnel. From the community's perspective, the company's actions help improve the fundamental core of the area. When the information is publicized, it relays an important message and sets the pace for other companies to follow suit.

According to the Business for Social Responsible Community Relations, "community relations refers to a wide range of actions taken by companies to maximize the impact of the donated money, time, products, services, influence, management knowledge, and other resources on the communities in which they operate" (Corporate Social Solutions, 2000).

Community relations is when a corporation tries to meet the requirements and demands of society and its surrounding community. By making this commitment to the community, a corporation receives an improved reputation, and stronger employee and customer loyalty.

The 1999 Cone/Roper Trends Report states that 94 percent of the surveyed Americans have a more positive image of companies that associate themselves with community causes. In addition, 79 percent are more likely to switch brands and 77 percent would switch to retailers that associate themselves with a cause. Therefore, a strong reputation for community goodwill increases customer loyalty and satisfaction.

The Trend Report also states that community relations affects current and future employees. Of the employees of companies that are involved with a cause, 90 percent feel proud of their company's values opposed to 55 percent without cause programs; 87 percent feel a strong sense of loyalty opposed to 67 percent without cause programs and more than half of American workers wish their employers would do more to support a social cause. Therefore, companies must adopt cause programs in order to stay competitive when recruiting and retaining qualified employees.

How Does One Become a "Neighbor of Choice?"

A company must build and maintain positive relationships in its community, as well as handle community issues and concerns with sincerity in order to become a "neighbor of choice." Fundamentally, the community program must improve the quality of community life and deal with the long-term business goals of the corporation by following these guidelines:

1. The company must write a community relations vision statement to recognize the community issues that have a direct relationship to the corporation and its success. The vision statement must be comprehensive throughout the organization and represent the company's commitment to being a neighbor of choice.
2. The company must focus this commitment on issues that relate to the company's business goals and services. This enables the neighbor of choice strategy to become an essential part of the company's corporate culture. This also helps

define the commitment and permits it to guide major business decisions.
3. The chief executive and/or key officer of the organization must be in continuous contact with the community through speeches and employees by memo to demonstrate the company's commitment to the community.
4. Human and financial resources must be allocated. This includes giving departmental status to community relations, involving employees at all levels and involving an outside community relations source.
5. Employee involvement is key to making the strategy a success. Volunteerism on the part of the employee must be rewarded in some way, acknowledging employee involvement in community issues.
6. Finally, all information regarding a company's community involvement should be published in both internal and external sources. This allows the employees and the community to see the results of a company's community relations strategy.

LESSON ELEVEN: FINDING THE LEADER IN YOU

There is no question that there is a perception that leadership styles are different amongst women and men; studies have been done on this for decades. Schein ran a study in 1973, which was again conducted in 1980, and then it was again replicated by Meyers in 1999; men were found to be "concerned about independence, direct, competitive and solution oriented," whereas women were discovered to be "concerned about relationships, cooperative, process oriented and indirect when it came to leadership styles."

Today, more studies have shown that men and women lead differently, but what is perhaps of most relevance is that not only are there differences, but those characteristics held by men are often seen as the characteristics associated with successful leaders. When looking at all the barriers women must face to reach top-level management, the question arises of how did that 5 percent reach the top.

Although there are several answers, including going above and beyond the expectations placed on them as one of the highest reasons, I have a different philosophy on how we will rise to the top: WE MUST HELP ONE ANOTHER GET THERE!!!

Barbara Walters recently said, "I have interviewed perhaps all the great leaders of our time and just as those before them, their time too ends." So leadership can be for decades or it can be for one instant; one moment in time that one person's leadership changes the course of history. Alice Paul standing in front of the gates of the White House, refusing to move and being arrested, which lead to the passage of the 19th Amendment, enabling Women to vote. Rosa Parks refusing to sit in the back of the bus in 1955, leading to the civil rights movement.

Minorities and Women Find Understanding the Contracting Process and Identifying Opportunities Challenging

Learning about contracting opportunities and understanding the contracting process is still a big hurdle for small business owners, especially for minorities and women. Minorities were more interested in obtaining contracts than their Caucasian counterparts, at 35 percent to 27 percent, respectively.

Women also indicated a stronger interest in contracting than men – women at 63 percent versus men at 37 percent.

Over a quarter (27 percent) of the business owners surveyed are not interested in corporate or government contracts and approximately 16 percent of the respondents have entered their company into the CCR database, which is the federal government's central database used to support federal contract opportunities.

More than half of the respondents indicate that they don't expect to engage in contracting with state or federal government markets in the next five years.

I have spoken to women in business all over the country, and also internationally, and I hear similar statements about us being the "minority." This is what I have told women across the globe: Women are not the minority. I repeat, we are not the minority. It is our responsibility to teach our children well; daughters, sons, nieces, grandchildren.

It is paramount for us to teach our sons the importance of respecting women in and out of the business arena and the importance of an equal playing field. It is also important to teach our daughters to respect themselves to reach the potential that God has outlined for them in his master plan, whatever that may be. It is also our responsibility as women to make change and not sit idly by.

We need to speak out and help one another, mentor and build up other women in business.

I hope that one day we can be known as CEOs of our successful companies rather than win recognition for the adversity we needed to overcome to become successful women business owners

LESSON TWELVE: GET THE HELP!

Help Is Out There
More than 2700 chambers of commerce are located throughout the country and other similar organizations are located globally.

In the US, the Small Business Administration has offices in nearly every major city and there are a variety of FREE counseling, training and information services, including the Service Corps of Retired Executives (SCORE), Business Information Centers (BICS) and Small Business Development Centers (SBDC). In addition, procurement center representatives can be found at each major military installation.

You Are in Business
Finally, as Dorothy Parker said, "The most beautiful words in the English language are 'Check enclosed.'" You are in business to make a profit!

When you go into business for yourself, always remember to put processes in place to protect your company and your assets.

Some of the best advice I ever received was from an accountant who told me to pay myself first. We, as women, tend to put everyone ahead of ourselves. There is everything right about respecting your talents, surrounding yourself with the right resources, developing your business and marketing plan, investing in networking and marketing to grow your business. There is nothing wrong in tooting your own horn a bit so others know your accomplishments; or better yet, let others toot it for you. However, make some noise.

To succeed, all of the books and those who are already there will tell you, "Love what you do". It is true.

Don't try to take on the worries of the world on your shoulders; take care of you first. You know, if the plane is going down, put the oxygen mask on yourself first, or if the ship is sinking, put the flotation device on first, otherwise you will crash or drown and be of no value to anyone. It is the same with business; first and foremost, take care of yourself so you are financially strong enough to take care of your employees and others, be persistent and, most of all, "Believe in yourself, follow your dream and make it happen!"

EPILOGUE: 7 KEYS OF SUCCESSFUL WOMEN IN BUSINESS

1: Be Not Afraid

Eleanor Roosevelt said, "You must do the thing you fear the most."

Successful women in business act quickly and decisively. They do not fear the possibility of failure. They move forward toward their goal, even when faced with obstacles and adversity. And when they do come across a situation that does not go as planned, they do not sweat it, dwell on it or lose their confidence; they take it as a lesson learned, which strengthens them for the next challenge.

2: Master the Mind Alliance

No one can be successful without the help of others. Successful women know that in order to achieve a successful outcome, it is imperative to build solid relationships. They surround themselves with knowledgeable professionals and talented employees, knowing this collaboration will ultimately create a healthy environment and successful outcomes.

3: Follow Your Gut

Successful women in business have learned to use their intuition to their advantage in business dealings. A woman's intuitive nature has been proven to be more in tune than that of her counterpart's. In other words, listen to your gut and go with it!

4: Service Is Leadership

When women reach a certain level of success, they immediately begin to pay forward. One very important component of leadership is service and mentorship. Women who mentor other women are creating an opportunity for positive change in the workplace and they create a great support system for themselves.

5: Yes Means Yes and No Means No

Women who are successful in business have learned to be decision makers and stick with their decisions. They understand business is competitive and our counterparts have learned how to play the game well. Once they make their decision, they do not change their mind, or allow their mind to be changed.

6: The Art of Being Multi-Dimensional

Another advantage successful women have found is to take advantage of their ability to multi-task. Our counterparts are linear, finishing one project at a time before going on to the next. Women can use their natural ability as multi-taskers to handle various items simultaneously, moving on to the next and allowing for more projects.

7: The Great Communicators

Women use the art of communications to their advantage in business. Successful women set their goals. They also integrate their listening skills, instincts and empathy into their daily communication. We are just beginning to understand the mysterious ways in which the mind works, but successful people have long known how to use the power of creative vision to their advantage.

The Eureka Secret

Many "new" ideas are really nothing more than a new combination of two well-known products or ideas. Nevertheless, great fortunes have been built upon such combinations when they are supported by a clever name and marketing campaign. Use your imagination and never limit yourself. Unlearn what you have learned that has caused any fear or trepidation toward competitiveness, follow your instincts, align yourself with like-minded people who are positive, energetic, supportive and knowledgeable, set your goals, give back and, most of all, use your voice to find your Eureka moment; it is possible!

"Something which we think is impossible now is not impossible in another decade."
Constance Baker Motley
(First black woman in the US to become a Federal Judge)

My hope is that women will begin to more readily share their lessons learned and use their voice. That they will ask one another for advice and give each other advice, make the connections and start breaking down the fences that separate us from that equal playing field.

"We ask justice, we ask equality, we ask that all the civil and political rights that belong to citizens of the United States, be guaranteed to us and our daughters forever."
Susan B. Anthony, Declaration of Rights for Women, July 1876

FURTHER INFORMATION

People QuickFacts	USA
Population, 2011 estimate	311,591,917
Population, 2010	308,745,538
Population, percent change, 2000 to 2010	9.7percent
Population, 2000	281,421,906
Persons under 5 years, percent, 2010	6.5percent
Persons under 18 years, percent, 2010	24.0percent
Persons 65 years and over, percent, 2010	13.0percent
Female persons, percent, 2010	50.8percent
White persons, percent, 2010 (a)	72.4percent
Black persons, percent, 2010 (a)	12.6percent
American Indian and Alaska Native persons, percent, 2010 (a)	0.9percent
Asian persons, percent, 2010 (a)	4.8percent
Native Hawaiian and Other Pacific Islander, percent, 2010 (a)	0.2percent
Persons reporting two or more races, percent, 2010	2.9percent
Persons of Hispanic or Latino origin, percent, 2010 (b)	16.3percent
White persons not Hispanic, percent, 2010	63.7percent

Living in same house 1 year & over, 2006-2010	84.2 percent
Foreign born persons, percent, 2006-2010	12.7 percent
Language other than English spoken at home, pct age 5+, 2006-2010	20.1 percent
High school graduates, percent of persons age 25+, 2006-2010	85.0 percent
Bachelor's degree or higher, pct of persons age 25+, 2006-2010	27.9 percent
Veterans, 2006-2010	22,652,496
Mean travel time to work (minutes), workers age 16+, 2006-2010	25.2
Housing units, 2010	131,704,730
Homeownership rate, 2006-2010	66.6 percent
Housing units in multi-unit structures, percent, 2006-2010	25.9 percent
Median value of owner-occupied housing units, 2006-2010	$188,400
Households, 2006-2010	114,235,996
Persons per household, 2006-2010	2.59
Per capita money income in past 12 months (2010 dollars) 2006-2010	$27,334
Median household income 2006-2010	$51,914
Persons below poverty level, percent, 2006-2010	13.8 percent

Business QuickFacts	USA
Private nonfarm establishments, 2009	7,433,465
Private nonfarm employment, 2009	114,509,626
Private nonfarm employment, percent change 2000-2009	0.4percent
Nonemployer establishments, 2009	21,090,761
Total number of firms, 2007	27,092,908
Black-owned firms, percent, 2007	7.1percent
American Indian- and Alaska Native-owned firms, percent, 2007	0.9percent
Asian-owned firms, percent, 2007	5.7percent
Native Hawaiian and Other Pacific Islander-owned firms, percent, 2007	0.1percent
Hispanic-owned firms, percent, 2007	8.3percent
Women-owned firms, percent, 2007	28.8percent
Manufacturers' shipments, 2007 ($1000)	5,338,306,501
Merchant wholesaler sales, 2007 ($1000)	4,174,286,516
Retail sales, 2007 ($1000)	3,917,663,456
Retail sales per capita, 2007	$12,990
Accommodation and food services sales, 2007 ($1000)	613,795,732

Building permits, 2010	604,610
Federal spending, 2009	3,175,336,050[1]
Geography QuickFacts	**USA**
Land area in square miles, 2010	3,531,905.43
Persons per square mile, 2010	

(http://quickfacts.census.gov/qfd/states/00000.html)

REFERENCE SOURCES

Government Contractor's Resource Guide (2010)
White House Women & Girls Counsel (2011)
Women's Bureau Center for Women's Business Research (2007/2008/2009/2010)
Guardian Life Small Business Research Institute (2009)
Center for Women's Business Research and National Women's Business Council. The Economic Impact of Women-Owned Businesses in the United States (2009)
US Bureau of the Census. (2002/2010)
Million Dollar Strategies from Women Owners of $1 Million Plus Firms (Fact card)
Kauffman, The Foundation of Entrepreneurship
Women Business Owners and Growth Capital

ABOUT THE AUTHOR

Ms. Daisy Gallagher is the founder and CEO/chief global strategy officer of Gallagher & Gallagher Worldwide (GGW). GGW is a 21-year-old award-winning strategic integrated marketing communications agency that specializes in defense and civilian contracting, focusing on strategic marketing, recruitment branding, public information and top-level event deployment. The firm has been named one of the top 10 agencies by the Business Journal and has received more than 100 industry awards.

Ms. Gallagher has been acclaimed by peers at the highest levels of professional accomplishment. Among her many awards and recognitions are: Public Relations Society of America's Overall Excellence Awards for two consecutive years; one of the Top 5 Women-Owned Businesses in the Nation; Woman-Owned Business of the Year (President's Award); Businessperson of the Year (SBA); Women In Communication (WIC) Award for Public Relations; European American Women's Council (EAWC) ARTEMIS Award.

In addition, Ms. Gallagher has received numerous citations and recognitions from congress, state and local governments and community groups for her leadership, business acumen and community involvement.

Prior to founding GGW, Ms. Gallagher started her career at Avon International corporate headquarters in Manhattan where she worked for eleven years, quickly rising to managerial level. At the peak of her career, she made a decision to leave the corporate world and relocate to rural America to provide a better quality of life for her son, who developed a chronic illness, which ultimately left him with a disability. When her son's illness was diagnosed as environmental, she became more involved with sustainability and diversity causes and initiatives.

Ms. Gallagher is recognized as a leading national expert in sustainable marketing and event logistics deployment. She serves as senior advisor on many initiatives and as the lead organizer and advisor for the World Green Energy Symposium (WGES), and other sustainability congresses. Her company has been awarded Platinum-Level Green Business Certification by the Green Business Bureau.

Ms. Gallagher has appeared on television and radio and been featured in major media across the country and internationally, including Forbes and Business Week. She is the author/editor of several books, including The Government Contractor's Resource Guide, which is used by numerous federal contracting officers and contractors, as well as in several universities.

This is her latest book, a title she held for many years until her intuition told her the timing was right to unveil it. How to Succeed In a Testosterone World Without Losing Estrogen highlights the challenges, obstacles and lessons for woman in business. It is a must read for every woman and man who is interested in empowering women.

This book is loaded with facts, statistics and indispensible lessons learned over 30 years as a successful woman in business to strengthen women in the business world whether they are a startup or are seasoned and feel stuck in the middle of the pack. You will learn the challenges women face and her common sense solution posed along with the many opportunities available to the workplace when women have an equal seat at the table and share equally in leadership opportunities in the workplace.

GGW was the first woman-owned and the first Latina-owned business to be awarded the GSA AIMS schedule. Ms. Gallagher was appointed by the White House and unanimously confirmed by Congress to serve on the Federal Small Business Advisory Committee. She was also appointed to serve on the GSA Industry-Government Council Steering Committee and the GSA Industry-Government Council.

She has been featured as a success story and as an expert on branding and sustainable marketing initiatives and best practices, addressing her peers as a keynote speaker on a PBS broadcast. She has also been a keynote and lecturer for private and public industry, for the US Department of Defense, US Department of Energy, the Small Business Administration (SBA), the NIH Federal Mentoring Roundtable, and the US General Services Administration (at several GSA Industry Days in Washington, DC and at GSA Training Expos). Internationally, Ms. Gallagher has addressed large audiences at the Foreign Ministry of Greece on Branding and has spoken at the United Nations.

She was highlighted as a success story by GSA for the USPS Branding Initiatives and as a featured keynote for women's organizations, such as Women Impacting Public Policy, the National Association of Women Business Owners, European-American Women's Council and others. Her firm is a certified minority woman-owned business and was certified as an SBA Hubzone in 2000.

As a long-standing defense and civilian contractor, Ms. Gallagher has overseen recruitment branding, public affairs, event deployment and integrated marketing campaigns for more than 22 federal agencies, including the Department of Defense (Army, Navy, Air Force, Pentagon), Department of Veterans Affairs, Department of Justice, Department of Health & Human Services, USPS, Department of Energy, General Services Administration and the White House. In addition to her US government work, she has also consulted for many Fortune 500 corporations, as well as for state and local governments, private industry and non-profits.

Ms. Gallagher earned an Advanced Master's in project management from Villanova University and holds several post-graduate certificates in fields such as executive leadership and crisis management; she also holds a certification as a project management professional. She also attended Harvard Business School and is trained in NLP, a certified success coach and a board certified clinical practitioner (CHT).

www.ingramcontent.com/pod-product-compliance
Lightning Source LLC
Chambersburg PA
CBHW030901180526
45163CB00004B/1656